What People Are Saying About
The 10-Step Empowerment Series

"Through the use of introspective questions, the book invites the reader to take a journey of self-examination in order to accept the loss and to reengage in life."

—Ian Landry, MA, MSW, Case Manager

"Bevan has real-life experience in the area of loss and "rebuilding" her life and self-esteem in the face of traumatic experiences such as being abandoned by a partner."

—Margaret M. Mustelier, PsyD

"Nowadays, there are too many books about adult loving relationships, but they usually are generic and abstract descriptions. This book is different because it moves to specificity and provides concrete steps to overcome a disrupting episode in our lives."

—Carlos J. Sanchez, MA, Family Therapist

"Lynda Bevan delivers what she promises in the title of the book: it is a practical guide and a no-nonsense approach. Her descriptions of the experiences are palpable."

—Chin Tao, LMFT

"This is a well thought out, useful little book that is an excellent guide for those recovering from a broken long-term relationship."

—Robert Rich, MSc, PhD, MAPS

"The book is studded with illuminating case studies and provides an excellent exposition of issues such as post-traumatic emotional responses, pre-trauma expectations, setting boundaries, forgiveness and acceptance, and the do's and don'ts of moving forward. A gem."

—Sam Vaknin, PhD
author *Malignant Self Love: Narcissism Revisited*

"Bevan provides practical steps to help a person begin the process of change, and during that process, to decide how the relationship will be affected, and whether to stay in the relationship, based on how your partner reacts to your new behaviors."

—Tyler R. Tichelaar, PhD
Author of *The Marquette Trilogy*

"This easy to relate to, solution-focused guide does not attempt to push an agenda; it simply provides a foundation of understanding along with the tools necessary to begin trusting one's own feelings again. Bevan dedicates great thought toward realistic problem solving approaches while maintaining a focus on safety, health, and growth."

—Erin M. Hudges, LCSW, *Rebecca's Reads*

When I was in college, I outlined all my lectures and readings so I could easily go back and study those points of importance without being bogged down with extraneous detail. That is what this book is — a detailed outline and explanation of how jealousy and envy in a relationship can be recognized and dealt with. It is a step-by-step guide into the psychology behind the emotions and a program to change them.

—Enid Grabner, *Rebecca's Reads*

Overcoming Guilt
A Practical Guide

Lynda Bevan

Loving Healing Press

Overcoming Guilt: A Practical Guide
Copyright © 2014 by Lynda Bevan. All Rights Reserved
Book #6 in the 10-Step Empowerment Series

Library of Congress Cataloging-in-Publication Data

Bevan, Lynda.
  Overcoming guilt : a practical guide / by Lynda
Bevan.
      pages cm -- (The 10-step empowerment series ;
bk. 6)
  Includes bibliographical references and index.
  ISBN 978-1-61599-222-5 (pbk. : alk. paper) -- ISBN
978-1-61599-223-2 (ebook)
  1. Guilt. 2. Shame. I. Title.
  BF575.G8B48 2014
  152.4'4--dc23
                                        2014001654

Distributed by: Ingram Book Group

Published by:
Loving Healing Press
5145 Pontiac Trail
Ann Arbor, MI 48105-9627

info@LHPress.com   www.LovingHealing.com
Tollfree 888-761-6268   Fax 734-663-6861

THE 10-STEP EMPOWERMENT SERIES

- Life After Your Lover Walks Out (2006)
- Life After Betrayal (2007)
- Stop Being Pushed Around! (2008)
- Life Without Jealousy (2009)
- How To Forgive (2011)
- Overcoming Guilt (2014)

About our Series Editor, Robert Rich, PhD

Loving Healing Press is pleased to announce Robert Rich, PhD as Series Editor for the *10-Step Empowerment Series*. This exciting new series conveys practical guides written by seasoned therapists for solving real-life problems.

Robert Rich, MSc, PhD, MAPS, AASH is a highly experienced counseling psychologist. His website www.anxietyanddepression-help.com is a storehouse of helpful information for people suffering from anxiety and depression.

Bob is also a multiple award-winning writer of both fiction and non-fiction, and a professional editor. His writing is displayed at www.bobswriting.com. You are advised not to visit him there unless you have the time to get lost for a while.

Three of his books are tools for psychological self-help: *Anger and Anxiety: Be in charge of your emotions and control phobias, Personally Speaking: Single session email therapy,* and *Cancer: A personal challenge.* However, his philosophy and psychological knowledge come through in all his writing, which is perhaps why three of his books have won international awards, and he has won many minor prizes. Dr. Rich currently resides at Wombat Hollow in Australia.

Contents

Introduction

How many of you will own up to feeling guilty about something or someone in your past or now? Guilt is a word that can bring about deep feelings of loss, horror, anger, shame, and helplessness. Guilt is an emotional destroyer hell-bent on causing chaos and misunderstanding.

Everyone has felt guilty at some time. Guilt is a state of mind that will destroy love and create suffering. Guilt is what you get when you cannot forgive yourself for something you have thought, said, or done. Guilt is how you feel when you believe you have made a mistake. This guilt you absorb seems to be caused by what you did; but this is not necessarily true. Guilt is caused by how you react to what you did. You put yourself through inner torture, asking yourself, 'Why couldn't I have done more?' or 'Why did I do what I did?' You beat yourselves up with all these questions and *if onlys*'. Feeling guilty reinforces your feelings of not being right with yourself and not having done the right thing at that time. This results in loss of confidence and self-respect. Fortunately, because you were/are the one who has created the guilt, you can also let it go and move on.

In order to begin the process of moving on from guilt, we have to acknowledge that we live our life doing the very best we can with the limited knowledge and understanding we have at any given time. You are not born with the awareness and skills to deal with emotional issues in a positive way, and as a direct result of this fact, we make mistakes. But you must remember that you only learn lessons from the mistakes you make Making mistakes is perfectly normal and part of the learning process. Turning a mistake into an advantage is the key to moving forward with awareness and wisdom. A popular saying is, *you are always wise in hindsight*, after you learn the lesson!

In order to move on from guilt, you have to first of all forgive yourself for not knowing any better, for not being wiser back there at that time. This book takes a good look at guilt, the cause and the damage done as a result of you not knowing and understanding more than you did at that time. It is a difficult journey, but a journey not to be missed.

Step 1 – What Is 'Guilt?'

'Guilt' is primarily an *emotion* experienced by people who believe they have done something wrong. Guilt is an affective state in which one experiences *conflict* at having done something one believes one should not have done (or, conversely, not having done something one believes one should have done). It gives rise to a feeling that does not go away easily and is driven by *conscience.*

Guilt is a destructive, powerful emotion linked to shame. You judge yourself by trying to live by standards dictated to you from your early-learning role models and your environment, your culture, and from the belief system that you have brought with you into adulthood. Some of these beliefs are out of date and inaccurate, having been indoctrinated into all your life in order to maintain control during your childhood.

Before you feel guilty, you have to say or do something that your belief system identifies is wrong. If you believe something you said or did was wrong, it might be because you have been brainwashed with a code of behavior that was passed on to you during your childhood. In today's culture, it is possible that your code of behavior might be considered old-fashioned and inappropriate. During childhood, you are dependent on your role models to show you what is right and what is wrong, and the answer to this question, and other questions, forms your basic belief system. But what if the information that is passed to you is wrong or outdated? What happens is that you still believe it. You accept, without question, the stuff that pops into your head and stick to it, believing it to be right.

Everyone is familiar with 'guilt.' If you don't have a conscience, then you won't feel guilty (sociopath). Guilt is what you feel when you believe you are responsible for an action or statement that you now regret.

How is Guilt Classified?

True guilt is the guilt you feel when you know you have said or done something that goes against your moral code of conduct.

False guilt is the guilt you will feel even when you have done nothing wrong at all. It feels like shame, even though you have no idea why it is that you feel ashamed.

Negative feelings resulting from social and/or personal causes act as 'breeders' of guilt. Thus, one may harbor guilt associated with shame, embarrassment, and/or humiliation.

Here are some examples of why you feel guilty:

You feel guilty when you believe you are responsible for any set of circumstances that you are or were involved in;

- You feel guilty when you have a strong (moral) belief in right and wrong that hinders your enjoyment in doing something you want/wanted to do;

- You feel guilty when you take responsibility for someone else's problems;
- You feel guilty when you look back on your life and regret having done or said something;
- You feel guilty because of an irrational belief;
- You feel guilty when you have said or done something to someone who is now dead;
- You feel guilty when you believe you are responsible for stuff you are definitely not responsible for.

An example of a mother's guilt:

I have counseled many women who have left their partners/ husbands for one reason or another, and most of these women have felt very guilty that they have taken their child/children from their Dad and the home the family once shared. Weeks, months, and years later, the guilt can remain the same. In fact, as the years roll by, the guilt of divorce can increase. A lady who was referred to me by her General Practitioner had left her ex-husband, the father of her two children, some 18 years ago and still felt the tug of guilt in the pit of her stomach. She tried to overcompensate her guilt by being there, purchasing items, and doing all manner of things for her children. She truly believed that she had caused her children deep emotional pain by leaving her husband, their father.

This lady compared herself to her peers who had sustained their marriages and relationships and who were now entering midlife and retirement together. She craved the normality of having remained faithful and committed to one partner. She felt she was a failure and believed that she should have stayed in the marriage for the sake of the children. During one session, she brought along her eldest daughter and asked me if it was possible for her daughter to join in the session. I agreed.

During the session, the issue of her divorce and the resulting feelings with regard to her children was discussed. Her daughter was amazed by her mom's revelations and wholeheartedly disagreed, saying that she remembered when she was a young teenager witnessing her father's behavior toward her mom and followed her mom, when she went into the kitchen, and said to her mom, "Why don't you tell Dad to go because he treats you badly?"

'Guilt'—the word sounds ugly, doesn't it? It is a word that carries with it the most terrible, haunting feelings that stick to you like glue. The questions you ask yourself cannot be answered by you on a rational level. You are burdened with the deed and the word, and you feel you cannot escape or even believe that you don't deserve to be free of the feeling of guilt. You hang on to guilt as if by some illusion feeling guilty makes you atone for your misdeeds.

Here are some examples of the questions you ask yourself if you feel guilty:

- Why couldn't I have done more?
- Why did I do what I did?
- Why did I say that?
- Why didn't I see what was going to happen?
- Why have I got to live with these feelings?
- Why didn't I wait longer before leaving as I did?
- Why didn't I lock the car?
- Why did I drive too fast?
- Why did I run away?
- Why didn't I say goodbye when I had the chance?
- Why didn't I take him/her to the doctor sooner?
- Why didn't I take the chance/opportunity when I was offered it?
- Why have I got to put up with this?
- Why did I cheat?
- Why did I lie?
- What have I done that makes my life so awful?
- What have I done that is bad and is the cause of making my life such a constant struggle?

Guilt is an unpleasant emotional feeling that sticks to you like glue. It will never go away until you forgive yourself for that which you feel guilt about.

Here are some examples of where guilt comes from:

- Knowing you have said or done something wrong;
- Knowing that you have said or done something inappropriate;
- Your childhood role models, environment;
- Your early learning experiences at school, with friends and family;
- Your religious beliefs;
- Blame put on you by another person.

I am sure you can add to this list.

Whatever the circumstances of your guilt, you are left with feelings of remorse and shame. One of the main reasons you carry guilt is that when you look back, you can see that you could have done more; you could have handled a situation or a person differently; the outcome could have been so different, probably better, who knows? The fact is that you can't turn back the clock and re-do anything. You *have to* accept what you did, said, and believed and decide to let go of the guilty feeling and move on. The emotional weight of guilt is a burden which is extremely heavy and you don't want it anymore.

An Example of Guilt

A man I knew was very guilty because he was having a romantic and sexual affair behind his wife's back. This was bad enough; but to add to his guilt, he believed that God would cast him out of heaven for this act of betrayal. He was a religious man and attended church services every Sunday regular as clockwork. He held quite a senior position in the church and helped out whenever he could. The congregation and the Preacher thought very highly of him, which added to his feelings of remorse. The problem was that he genuinely loved the woman who had walked into his life some 13 years previously. He believed that she was his twin soul—kind, loving, caring, thoughtful, sincere, supportive, and helpful. Indeed, all the traits that others had remarked, he had himself.

'What could he do?' he asked himself. He had never felt this way before and didn't want to lose this woman he loved so much. He lived for the times that they could be together (which amounted to half-an-hour once a month). They would meet in a safe environment and make love together. He had never experienced such passion and openness. The sexual relationship they had answered all his fantasies and dreams. He telephoned this lady twice a week and realized that he could say anything to her. He was open and confided all his problems, feelings, fears, worries to 'his' woman, for this is what he called her. He had been unable to share these things with his wife. His wife, I later learned, was a bit of a cold fish, unresponsive, lacking in passion, and unforgiving. She regularly 'put him down' and humiliated him in front of family and friends. He had told her not to do that, of course; but she believed that she was always right and wouldn't consider the possibility that she was wrong in anything she said or did.

This couple had been married more that 35 years, but he admitted that there was never passion between them. Sex was rigid and inflexible, and he believed that his wife was just 'glad to get it over with'. This man was referred to me for counseling by his doctor because he was due for retirement, and he found it very difficult not only to come to terms with his retirement but also because this would ultimately mean that he could no longer see 'his' woman. The reason for this was that his wife was very controlling in the marriage and would make sure that he did what he was told and went where she demanded that he go. He was tied in, trapped with no visible escape. He was distraught. He knew that his relationship with this woman would have to end and he just couldn't come to terms with that thought. What would his life be like without her in it? Who could he talk to in the future the way he could talk to her? He didn't even try to answer these questions, preferring to bury his head in the sand and hope that the situation would work out in the end.

The weight of this secret was heavy on his heart. He wanted to leave his wife but felt he could not do this because of his faith. 'Thou shall not commit adultery'; he had, he was committing it, and he hated himself for doing this. 'His' woman helped him all she could. She tried everything to comfort him and even suggested he should talk to his Preacher to have some support and advice on what to do. He balked at this suggestion as he believed that his Preacher would tell him to 'drop the woman' and be a good husband to his chosen partner. He couldn't go through with this suggestion. Every Sunday he went to church and sat there feeling unworthy of being amongst God-fearing folk. He couldn't pray. He believed that he had no right to God's ear because he was a sinner who continued to sin. How did this situation end?

It hasn't. He continues to live with his head in the sand and hang on to the hope that 'his woman' would continue to wait for him and see him whenever he could escape from the prison that was his home. Even today, this man goes through the motions of living his life, constantly thinking of how it could be and how it should be. What was holding this man back from being with the woman he loved? Was it his religious beliefs? Was it because he would have felt ashamed? Was it because he believed that his family and friends wouldn't like him anymore? Was he afraid of experiencing change in his life?

I had and still have no answers to all these questions. Many months after his retirement, I saw him briefly once. He told me that he was trying to make the best of his life and his decision was to put his faith and his children (all in their 30s) before himself. In other words, he 'martyred' himself and continues to be unhappy, unfulfilled, and still guilty."

What are Your Negative Beliefs when You Feel Guilty?

You believe that...

- You cannot stick to the rules;
- You can decide to ignore the feelings of guilt for as long as you can (burying your head in the sand);
- You can decide not to feel guilty, believing guilt is for fools;
- You are above having feelings of guilt because you are always right in all that you do;
- You can make excuses for yourself in order to assuage your guilt;

- You should blame someone else for your deeds and resulting guilt;
- You will continue hurting and punishing yourself endlessly;
- You should hate yourself;
- God will punish you.

There are many more that I am sure you can think of. The list is different for each of you. Just like every other emotion, there is a positive as well as a negative side to guilt.

What are Your Positive Beliefs when You Feel Guilty?

You believe that...

- You must stop whatever it is you are doing that you believe is wrong;
- God loves you no matter what you are doing;
- You should love yourself;
- You believe in fate and should accept what happens to you;
- You can stick to the rules, and do so;
- You should face your fears and work through them;
- You should do the right thing and learn to live with the consequences.

Guilt can be pro-active as well as re-active. There is a negative and positive side to all emotion, and guilt is no exception.

Positive Guilt

Guilt used positively can be used to define the difference between right and wrong, moral and immoral. This type of guilt is important and essential to maintaining a moral code of living. The *Ten Commandments* is an example of a basic moral code for living. If you fall from grace by disregarding and disrespecting one of the Ten Commandments, you will be guilty of not adhering to the moral code set down for you by God. Your actions will be regarded as sinful and being sinful is a disgrace.

Here are some examples of positive guilt:

- Guilt demonstrates that you have a conscience;
- Guilt that has turned from negative to positive can make you closer to your partner (paying him/her more attention, and being mindful of their needs) ;
- Guilt helps you recognize when you have said or done something bad and gives you the opportunity to rectify the situation;
- If you have experienced guilt, you will be better placed to recognize this feeling in someone else, and you can empathize with this person and try to help them overcome their guilt feelings;
- Guilt allows you the opportunity to say sorry;
- Guilt allows you the opportunity to make amends for any wrongdoing;
- Guilt can provoke a change in your attitude, leading to more positive thinking;
- Guilt can provoke a change in your action and reaction;

- Guilt can motivate you to be sensitive to someone else's issues;
- Guilt can move you toward helping other people having guilt issues;
- Guilt can reinforce your doing things the right, moral way.
- All the above and there are many more examples.

What Can Negative Guilt Do to You?

Negative guilt is damaging to your overall wellbeing in a number of ways.

Here are some examples of what negative guilt can do to you:

- Guilt can make you physically unwell;
- Guilt can make you anxious;
- Guilt can make you depressed;
- Guilt can make you stressed;
- Guilt can make you sad;
- Guilt can make you obsessively conscientious to the point of continuously second-guessing yourself;
- Guilt can stop you from doing or saying something (in fear of doing or saying the wrong thing);
- Guilt can make you too sensitive to the needs of others to the point where you neglect yourself;
- Guilt can stop you from making decisions;
- Guilt can make you emotionally blocked.

Feelings of guilt may also be induced in you by the people around you.

Here are some examples how people make you feel guilty?

- People can make you feel guilty if you don't react to them in the way they want;
- People can make you feel guilty even when you know they are wrong;
- People can make you feel guilty by reinforcing your irrational beliefs;
- People can make you feel guilty by blaming you for something you did in your past or present;
- People or partners can make you feel guilty when they are not personally responsible for their actions;
- People can make you feel guilty when they are not accountable for their part in your relationship with them;
- People can make you feel guilty by their continual judgment on things you do and say;
- People can make you feel guilty by behaving like a 'victim' and expecting you to do things for them;
- People can make you feel guilty by being 'martyrs'.

Here are some examples of the things you say to yourself that reinforces feelings of guilt:

- I am bad and do not deserve to be happy;
- I am responsible for my family's happiness (there is some truth in this statement but you must remember you are not solely responsible for

providing your family's happiness; your partner is also responsible);

- I am responsible for my family's financial circumstances (there is some truth in this, but again you must remember that your partner is also responsible in regard to this. If your partner is at home, looking after the children, he/she will help you with financial circumstances by budgeting carefully);

- I am responsible for all the hurt and pain my family experiences;

- I am responsible for my children's behavior when it's bad (there is some truth in this; however, you can only do your best to teach your child manners and politeness; also you are only one part of the relationship and both partners are responsible);

- I am responsible for not giving my family good holidays;

- I am responsible for the way other people/partners treat me (you are only responsible for yourself);

- I am responsible for the way other people perceive me (always do the right thing, even sometimes to my own detriment);

- I am responsible for making sure my children do not suffer as I did when I was a child (Although it's a good intention, it becomes bad when you place unrealistic expectations on yourself to give more).

Step 2 – Understanding Different Types of Guilt

There are different types of guilt. I will attempt to explain each of these starting with 'I am not good enough' in this step and following through the list with subsequent steps:

- "I am not good enough"
- "I am too good;
- "I want something I shouldn't want;
- "How dare I;
- "I am being selfish;
- "If only;
- "I should be doing something else with my time;
- "I am guilty for not being guilty.

I Am Not Good Enough

How many times have you either said this yourself or heard someone else say it? 'I am not good enough' comes from having no self-esteem, no self-worth, and a low confidence level. 'I am not good enough' is a belief system that destroys your mental health, your relationships, and your lifestyle. How does this happen?

Where the idea "I am not good enough" can come from:

- From being put down, humiliated, or ridiculed by someone, like a partner and others, in your past;
- From negative work experiences;
- From your childhood experiences;
- From being bullied;
- From observing your early role models (parents, grandparents, brothers, sisters, aunts, uncles) and never measuring up;
- From your relationship with your partner;
- From a series of experiences that have ended badly out for you.

If you have consistently been ridiculed by your partner, family, friends, or colleagues, you will come to believe that you are not good enough. This will have a detrimental effect on your mental health, which in turn will sour your relationship with the people that have made this statement to you.

Even the most confident person will eventually feel undermined and inconsequential if they are the subject of consistent put-downs. It's like a slow brainwashing experience that is meant to devalue you, usually so that the person who is putting you down can take charge and have control over you. This is the worst kind of 'guilt' in my opinion as it suggests you are being manipulated so that your partner (or others) can reign supremely at your emotional expense.

The Perpetrator (the guilty one)

The person who feels guilty will use sentences such as:

- 'If you loved me, you would _____'
- 'I don't see why you just can't _____'
- 'Don't worry about me; I'll be ok'
- 'I don't believe you love me; prove it by _____
- 'I believe I have the right to do and say what I want and to hell with the consequences'

The perpetrator (the guilty one) uses these sentences to:

- Make their partners do stuff for them;
- Opt out of responsibility;
- Make a partner feel bad;
- Put pressure on their partner;
- Make you believe that you are being unreasonable;
- Get their own way at any cost;
- Make themselves feel good and powerful.

The perpetrators are using guilt as a weapon against you so that they can have their own way. Using guilt against your partner will destroy your relationship. Manipulating your partner through guilt says (non-verbally) that I will love you as long as you do what I say. It is the act of loving someone conditionally. It is the act of loving your partner by having negative power over them. What this can mean to a relationship is that the perpetrator is continually asking his/her partner to prove over and over, every day, that they love them by expecting them to do things that they should be doing themselves. Where there is guilt in a relationship, there is no trust. Projecting guilt onto your partner is causing pain to that person in the hope that they will succumb to your manipulation and do things your way.

What are some effects of projected guilt on the innocent partner?

- It will make your partner feel used;
- It will make your partner feel unappreciated;
- It will make your partner feel angry;
- It will make your partner feel devalued;
- It will make your partner question your love for him/her;
- It will make your partner do things that they do not want to do;
- It will make your partner feel pressurized;
- It will make your partner feel vulnerable;
- It will make your partner feel insecure in the relationship;
- It will make your partner feel they have to perform well at all times;
- It will make your partner withdraw from you;
- It will make your partner become less honest in the relationship he/she has with you;
- It will make your partner feel he/she has to protect himself/herself from the onslaught.

When do people use guilt as a weapon against their partner?

- When you feel threatened;
- If you feel unloved;
- If you feel unworthy;
- To make your partner (or others) suffer emotional pain;
- To make your partner feel vulnerable;
- To gain control in a relationship;
- To manipulate people;
- To make you feel good.

Guilt is never used as a display of love for your partner. It is always used in a negative, unproductive, disabling manner. Healthy relationships are balanced with both partners having equal power. A relationship such as this is honest and a safe place to be.

Consider these two questions:

- Are my feelings of guilt interfering with my life and my relationships?
- Am I willing to accept that I am being unreasonable and want to change the way I am thinking and behaving?

Life and relationships are neither black nor white. When you are entrenched with guilt, it will be difficult to let go; but as you practice and become successful in letting go, the guilt will fade away. You should attempt to 'manage your guilt' rather than allowing your 'guilt to manage you'.

The Innocent Partner

The innocent partner (the one who is on the receiving end of this projected guilt) might be blissfully unaware what their partner is consciously or unconsciously doing to them. This innocent person can remain in complete ignorance for a long time before 'the penny drops' and he/she either sees what is happening for themselves, or someone else points it out to them. To be continually used and manipulated in this way will contaminate and poison the relationship you have with your partner.

Step 3 – 'I Am Too Good'

The Innocent Partner Response

How can you be too good?

- When you say 'yes' to everyone;
- When you take on board stuff that you shouldn't take on;
- When you are overcompensating for your partner's lack of involvement in the relationship;
- When you are over-investing in the relationship;
- When your partner is coasting and you are doing all the work;
- By doing all these things, you will, if not already, feel washed out, used, and emotionally abused.

Is that enough reasons? If you accept all this that I have written, shouldn't you be asking yourself why you continue to do this stuff? Why not risk asking yourself. 'Is the relationship with your partner worth the sacrifices you make?'

You may want to ask yourself:

- Why do I continue being the partner that does everything?
- Am I afraid that if I don't do anything and everything my partner asks me to do, then he/she might leave me?
- Am I being unreasonable, expecting my partner to share some of the load?
- Do I resent doing all this stuff for my partner?
- Do I really want this relationship?
- What is holding me back?

What answers have you come up with? Now ask yourself, 'Am I really being truthful in my answers?' Go back and ask yourself these questions again. Just to be sure. If you have answered that you genuinely don't mind doing everything your partner asks of you, then read no further. Stay in your comfortable groove, which is identified as 'need to be needed' and don't moan about it. If, however, you have answered 'yes' to the questions, ask yourself, 'what am I going to do about it?'

Here are some decisions you might choose to make:.

- Decide to end the relationship;
- Decide that you are hurting too much for this relationship to continue in this way;
- Decide that you are worth more than your partner is prepared to give you (these three examples all result in the partnership splitting up) ;

- Decide to confront your partner with these issues;
- Decide to learn to understand why your partner behaves in this way and take the relationship forward from that point, i.e., toward mutual understanding and open communication;
- Decide to do nothing and remain the same (unproductive and inactive);
- You could decide to seek counseling to air your feelings with a therapist in order to clear and focus your mind.

> Love means never having to say you are sorry
>
> ~ Eric Segal

Overcoming Guilt

Now that you have made a plan, I will give you some ideas on how to implement your part of the plan.

Some things that could be a part of the process of changes:

- You can help your partner admit they have used guilt as a weapon against you;
- You can help your partner in trying to identify when he/she started feeling guilty;
- You can help your partner to forgive him/ herself;
- You can help your partner by reinforcing to him/her that he/she is human and being human means that you will make errors in life;

- You can help your partner by discussing, probably at length, the issues that he/she have identified regarding when he/she started feeling guilty and continue discussing these issues until your partner is ready to let them go;
- You can help your partner by addressing his/her negative thoughts;
- You can help your partner by changing the negative thoughts to positive thoughts;
- You can help your partner by showing your commitment to the plan;
- You can help your partner by being supportive, sensitive, and understanding
- You can help your partner by being honest about how you are feeling and coping with this process;
- You can help your partner by reassuring him/her that they have nothing to be afraid of;
- You can help your partner by forgiving him/her for past behavior;
- You can help your partner by agreeing not to bring up the manipulative, uncooperative behavior that has been against you;
- You can help your partner to show affection and care for the people he/she holds close;
- You can ask yourself 'what is it about me that makes me want to stay in this type of relationship?'

- You should take care of yourself first in order to ensure that you have the necessary energy to provide the support which will be required.

Take some time to address each issue and be realistic with regarding to timescales. This process done correctly will take a considerable time to come to fruition.

Here are some examples of questions that are appropriate for your partner (the perpetrator) to ask him/herself at this time:

- Which of my problems are in the forefront of my mind at the moment?
- What role do I believe I play in the problem?
- What exactly is it that I do or say to make this problem worse? (Be specific)
- What role does someone else play in this problem?
- How much of my time is spent thinking about this problem?
- How much guilt do I experience with regard to this problem?
- Have I exaggerated my part in the problem?
- How much have I exaggerated the problem?
- If I imagine that the problem was not mine at all and I played no relevant part in the problem, how much guilt would I feel then?

Next, here are some examples of how the innocent partner should deal with the guilt in the problem.

Your innocent partner should ask:

- 'Is this problem my doing?'
- 'Is it possible to overcome and deal with the problem?'
- 'Is this problem only mine?'
- 'Am I taking on someone else's problem?'
- 'Am I able to see the problem objectively and deal with the issue in this way?'

Confronting you (the perpetrator) and asking pertinent questions will help you decide if you are the problem. People are afraid to look at themselves closely on an emotional level and, as such, choose to stay the same because the fear of confronting their issues is too frightening for them.

Your partner (perpetrator) should ask him/herself:

- Am I afraid of confronting the problem?
- Am I afraid I won't be able to deal with the issues that might arise from confronting the problem?
- Am I able to step back from my fears?
- Am I able to identify the issue that causes the fear and change my negative thinking pattern which is underneath the fear?
- Do I believe that I deserve to be kind to myself?
- Do I believe that I deserve to have my partner and others be good to me?
- To overcome guilt, you must both look at yourself and your behavior closely. With support and encouragement, you can overcome guilt and move on.

The role and understanding of the innocent partner is a crucial part of the perpetrator's recovery. If there is no honest communication and commitment between you in the partnership, you will not be successful in achieving your objective. Time should be given to the innocent partner to allow him/her to come to terms with the emotional abuse that they have experienced within the relationship. Often when the innocent partner fully comprehends what has been happening to them as a result of the actions of the perpetrator, they can become angry, resentful, disappointed, and/or rebellious, and will need some time to lick their wounds and be productive in creating a future with the perpetrator.

Step 4 – 'I Want Something I Shouldn't Want'

Everyone wants something they shouldn't want at some time in their life. This becomes a problem when you get hooked into wanting something that is unrealistic, inappropriate, and belonging to someone else.

A General List of What You Might Want

Here are some examples of what most people might want:

- a better house (realistic);
- more money (realistic) ;
- expensive holidays (realistic);
- to raise children (realistic);
- a better job (realistic);
- someone else's husband (unrealistic);
- someone else's wife (unrealistic);
- happiness with no problems to deal with (unrealistic);
- success in your chosen career (realistic);
- your boss's job (realistic as long as the method you choose is honorable);
- to steal money (unrealistic);

- to be someone else (unrealistic);
- to murder someone (unrealistic).

Write down a list of the things you believe you shouldn't want and ask yourself why you shouldn't have them. Some of the items you list might be physically and financially attainable, but perhaps you have never thought yourself able or worthy enough to get them. Be realistic and take a good look at what you want. Perhaps you will feel able to share this list with your partner. This decision is up to you. Sharing this list with your partner might open up a whole new objective for your relationship.

On the list above, I have indicated what I believe is realistic to obtain and what I believe is unrealistic. However, wanting someone's husband or wife can be a realistic option if both of you want that to happen. I am not in favor of romantic affairs of the heart when one or both parties are married, but that's not to say that it doesn't happen and not to say that it's entirely unrealistic and unattainable.

On the list above I have indicated that stealing money, wanting to be someone else, and wanting to murder someone are unrealistic. I think we can take these three examples as unrealistic and that you all agree with me.

The only things that you shouldn't want are emotional and material things that belong to someone else. Even that isn't bad as it can push you to get what they have by honest means.

Example

A lady I met didn't know what she wanted in her life. Despite offering a range of possibilities and options, she still had no idea on exactly which road to take on her journey through life. She made one comment that opened up some possibilities; she said, 'I would like to have a diary like the one you have, which is filled with meetings and events'. This was the first step in her recognizing that she wanted something that she believed, at that time, she couldn't have. She wanted a full life. She wanted to be wanted. She wanted to make a difference. She wanted to be valued and sought after for her unique contribution. I asked her if she wanted to be in the caring profession and she said 'yes' I think I have a contribution to make in that area'. That lady is now a Social Worker with a very full calendar.

To begin the process of finding out what it is you want in your life, you only need to find a small ray of desire. I believe that we all have the capacity in us to find out what we would like our lives to be.

Hopes and Dreams

Think of a time when you had a dream about your future. Indulge yourself and dream this again but with your eyes open this time. Everyone has dreams of what they want for their future until obstacles crop up to stop you in your tracks. If you believe, like many, that there are 'no problems, only solutions', you will find a way around each obstacle you encounter. Fundamentally, you have to stick with it and not be put off by stuff that gets in the way of you achieving your dream. This is easier said than done.

Let's take a look at some of the things that crop up to stop you from achieving your dreams:

- Lack of money
- Lack of support (no partner or a selfish partner)
- Lack of appropriate education and training
- Lack of crèche facilities and child support
- Too tired because you are doing too much
- Lack enthusiasm and desire (it's slowly ebbed away)
- Need to earn money to maintain the family unit with no time to pursue wants, needs, and desires
- Too high expectations of self
- Too high expectations of others/partners
- No expectation of self
- No expectation of others/partners
- Limited or no family support
- Fear of trying
- Fear of failing
- Fear of success
- Fear of being ridiculed
- Lack of self-worth
- Lack of self-confidence

These are only some of the reasons given for abandoning dreams. Dreams can become a reality, provided they are achievable, i.e., if you dream that you want to become the Queen of England, you will definitely not have your dream realized unless you are of Royal descent or from the ranks of accepted aristocracy. I am tempted to include you want to be the

President of the United States of America, but this would be achievable if you have the education and political awareness, financial backing, etc. If you keep your dream realistic, then you have as much chance of arriving at a satisfactory outcome as anyone else in a similar situation.

Step 5 – 'How Dare I!'

- How dare you believe that you can have something good happen to you?
- How dare you believe that you can prosper?
- How dare you believe that your partner is loyal, honest, committed, and loves you?
- How dare you hope that one day you will have the life you believe you deserve

Why Do You Doubt?

Here are some reasons why you doubt:
- You believe nothing good can come your way;
- You believe you are disliked;
- You don't believe in yourself;
- You have no confidence or self-esteem;
- You have played the part of the victim and have become used to being made to look incapable;
- No one believes in you;
- Your comments have been consistently ignored;
- You have suffered from physical and emotional abuse.

Let's take a look at each of these reasons.

If You Believe Nothing Good Can Come Your Way

Believing that nothing good can come your way is the defeatists approach to living. If you don't aspire to achieve whatever it is you want to achieve, you will never get there. To enable you to allow good to come your way, you must change your negative belief pattern that has been ingrained in your mind for a very long time. To begin this process of changing your negative belief pattern, you can turn the sentence around from your negative belief to a positive belief: 'I believe good can come my way'. With practice saying this sentence, your mind will start to accept this statement and, as a result, you will begin to see how you can achieve your aim.

As many musicians, including Troels Abrahamsen, Echo & The Bunnymen, and others have pointed out: *'Nothing comes to those who wait.'* I have met many people who are waiting for the good life to happen for them. These people are living in the 'waiting room of life'. Life is something that happens to others and never to you. Why? Because you are waiting for it to happen instead of creating the life you want. Good can and will come your way when you choose to make the necessary changes.

Here are some examples of what you should do in order to change your thinking pattern:

Change your old negative thinking process to a new, positive thinking process. You can do this by stopping your negative thoughts as soon as you think them. For example, if your thought tells you that you will never amount to anything, immediately respond with the sentence, 'I can achieve success and happiness and I am going to do this'. What you are actually doing when you say this sentence is that you are killing off the negative thought process and replacing it with a healthy positive response. The more you do this, the less chance your negative thoughts will have to scupper your thoughts of happiness and success. Your mind is like a computer. It will repeat and repeat the same old garbage until you change the programming of your thoughts.

Stay alert to your mind chatter (your thoughts); don't let your negativity prevail.

Share your plan with your partner, family, and friends who can help support you whilst you are engaging in this process.

Don't worry if you are taking a long time to accomplish this task. Remember you have been thinking negative thoughts for a very long time, and it is unlikely that you will be able to turn your thought process around quickly.

Take your time with this task. Rushing into it will only end up with you feeling frustrated and giving up.

Surround yourself with positive people. You will find in doing this task that your old friends will no longer be in tune with the 'new you' that you are creating by changing your thought processes and might try to unconsciously sabotage your efforts and even ridicule your attempts. Negativity breeds negativity. Positivity attracts positivity.

Don't give up even though it might feel you will never get there. You will.

If You Believe You Are Disliked

A little girl was told repeatedly by her mother that her father's family disliked her. 'Why?' asked the child. 'Because you are pretty and clever and they are jealous of you,' was the reply. This little girl grew up believing that her father's family disliked her and, as a result of this belief, paid little attention to them and never became involved in any family celebrations that took place. She always stayed on the edge of any family reunions, believing that she was just being tolerated by her father's family.

Indeed it is fair to say that the little girl's father's family was quite a difficult, argumentative group of people, always squabbling over the silliest things. When they got together, they always managed to malign someone in the family. Much later on, when the little girl was about twenty years old, her cousin (on her father's side) experienced physical abuse from her new husband and separated from him. The little girl's cousin (whom I will call Ann) was lonely and upset and 'phoned her cousin for a chat in the hope that they could go out for a drink together. The little girl (who was no longer little, and I will name her Jenny) readily agreed to this suggestion; and the two young ladies gelled immediately and their friendship grew over the years.

Ann and Jenny, now over 40, are still friends to this day. This is an example of how receptive your mind is when you are young. You will believe anything your role models choose to tell you. You will copy and re-enact your role model's behavior, because you never doubt your parents when you are young and you know no better. When the little girl became an adult and experienced the friendship with her cousin flourish, she looked back and could not understand why she believed that all her father's family disliked her.

Here are some reasons why you believe that you are disliked:

- You have been told this repeatedly;
- You have been ignored;
- You believe you are ugly;
- You are never invited to join a group for an evening out;
- There is something about you that gets under the skin of others;
- You are successful;
- You are unsuccessful;
- You live in a poor area of town;
- You have a profession;
- You drive a flashy car.

As you can see, this list is endless and your list might be different, shorter or longer. So, what can you do about it? Again, we are back to your negative belief system and your negative responses to those around you. By changing your negative belief system (this is the stuff you talk to yourself about), you are opening up a whole new world for you to enjoy. Read and re-read this book until you completely absorb all the information that will enable you to turn your life around.

If You Don't Believe in Yourself

There is only one person who can change this belief and that is *you*. Take the 'bull by the horns' and look at this belief squarely in the face. Why don't you believe in yourself? What have you done that makes this belief stay embedded in your negative thought processes? What has happened to you for you to downgrade yourself in this way? Go back in your memory to the very beginning and identify why this thought ever entered your head. If you want to undertake this exercise with your partner, family member, or friend, do so, if it feels right for you to do this. Uncover your basic belief system. Be honest and really look at your earlier relationships and interactions with your parents, grandparents, brothers, sisters, friends. Are you able to identify why you don't believe in yourself. The negative thought process you have that makes you believe you are a hopeless case has resulted in you having a low self-esteem, low self-worth, and low confidence. Are you happy thinking and behaving in this way? Are you happy not having trust in your partner or loved ones when they tell you that you are a good guy/gal?

Here are some suggestions for what you should do:

- Change your thought process as I have explained earlier on in this Step;
- Start taking *baby steps* (small challenges) in order to raise your self-esteem;
- Never feel foolish and stupid when you are engaging in this process; there are a lot of people who have a low self-esteem;

- Learn to step out of the box and dare to be different, more co-operative, more flexible;
- Observe the way you are being treated by your partner/family/friends as a result of this change in your thinking processes.

Anything you say or do will result in a reaction and response from the person or people you are talking with. When you are becoming successful in changing your thought processes, you will be amazed at the reactions of these people. They will be somewhat dumbfounded and confused that you are beginning to be surer of yourself, and more assertive with more social skills.

If You Have Low Confidence or Self-Esteem

Confidence comes with practice. Self-esteem comes when you believe you are a whole person able to deal with issues that could crop up on life's journey. Learning to change your thought processes is an arduous task but once achieved, your confidence levels will significantly rise. Having positive thoughts and being confident is an important aspect of living a life of quality. No one has the right to put you down, humiliate you, embarrass you, and make you feel insignificant and unimportant. You have a right to be. You have a right to feel good when you have done or said something that has a good effect on someone else. Never allow anyone to control your behavior by using negative words to undermine your confidence.

If you believe someone is trying to put you down, don't just sit there and accept it. Challenge the person who is putting you down in a calm, controlled manner, and ask them to explain why they feel the need to do this to you. If you do this, you are turning the question around and making them accountable for their behavior. See how they like being challenged in this way.

If you believe that someone is trying to humiliate you, be prepared by visiting the scenario in your head (use your imagination) prior to meeting the person that regularly uses this method of control with you, and remember a conversation you have had with this person in the recent past, and try to change your original response to this person in that situation. By doing this, you are anticipating that a similar situation is most likely to occur and are preparing your 'stock phrase answers' to use for future discussions with this person. It's called being proactive. Forewarned is forearmed.

If you believe that someone is trying to embarrass you, speak up and challenge this person. Usually when you do this, the bully will back down. You only need to stand up for yourself a few times for the bully to understand that you are not going to put up with this behavior anymore.

If You Have Played the Part of The 'Victim' Too Long or Too Well

How you might be perceived by others when you are in the role of 'victim':

- Incapable of making decisions;
- Being unreliable;
- Taking everything for granted and not contributing in any way;
- Being weak and vulnerable;

- Someone who defers any problems to someone else.

If you have done any of the above, you are sending a clear message to your partner/family/friends that you are not responsible or accountable for anything in your life. If you are fed up with this feeling, then you are ready to accept changing the process of your negative belief patterns into positive belief patterns. Take a step forward and try to change even some of the smallest behavior that you have previously used. Any small step in the right direction will lift your spirits.

If No One Believes in You

In order for people to believe in you, they have to see visible signs that you trust yourself. If your partner or others do not believe in you, it is because you have not demonstrated that you believe in yourself. In fact, you have demonstrated the complete opposite, which is that you don't believe in yourself. What came first, the chicken or the egg?

Consider what might have happened during your early learning stage of emotional development:

- You might have been given a clear message that your views are stupid;
- You might have been ignored;
- You might have been humiliated;
- You might have been ridiculed;
- You might have been physically or sexually abused;
- You might have always had your own way;

- You might have had tantrums and always got your way via this route;

- You might have been spoiled rotten.

There are more examples that will be unique to each individual.

The way forward is to start believing in you. You can do this by changing one small thing about the way you react to people and situations. If you no longer view yourself as somebody who does not believe in themselves, other people will take your lead. In other words, change your behavior and act that you believe in yourself. 'Act Happy And You Become Happy'.

If You Have Been Consistently Ignored

You have to ask yourself why you are consistently ignored. People are usually only ignored because they are boring or because they have nothing to contribute, either to the conversation or the situation. To be recognized, you have to speak up and give your opinion on stuff that's happening. If you don't do this, people will learn not to ask you or involve you in any event or circumstances that develop. They will assume that you will go with the flow and agree to anything and everything that someone else voices. As I have already demonstrated earlier in this Step:

You must learn to believe that

- You are valued;

- You can change;

- You are important;

- You can contribute;

- You are confident;

- You are no longer a victim;
- You are capable.

When you demonstrate just one of the above list, then those people who are close to you will begin to reassess their opinion of you.

If You Have Been Physically or Emotionally Abused

If you have been physically and/or emotionally abused, you have suffered pain and inner turmoil and there is a strong possibility that you are stuck on your path of emotional development. If you haven't already had counseling, please do so. You will find it very useful and is the first step in moving on from this stuck state. In reading this book, you are already acknowledging that you are unhappy with yourself. Or, if your partner is reading this book, this means that he/she has recognized that there are significant changes that should be made in your relationship. With support from your partner, family, and friends, you can overcome your early childhood experiences and emerge a whole person who has got a lot to give. Your early negative experiences were horrendous to experience but having had this experience you will become a sensitive, aware person.

Step 6 – 'I Am Being Selfish'

Are you being selfish by:

- Not becoming involved with stuff that's going on around you?
- For opting out of responsibility?
- Be being a victim?
- Because you rely on your partner or others?
- Being unsupportive of your partner or others?
- Seeming uncaring?

There are a lot of issues to address about being selfish. I am of the opinion that *you* are being selfish. I don't believe for one second that you deliberately set out to be selfish. I believe that your lack of self-esteem, your background, etc, have deterred you from experiencing a positive emotional development path.

Try to answer these two fundamental questions. What does selfish mean to you? Is it wrong to be selfish?

Positive Selfishness

There is a positive and negative to every emotion. Being selfish in a positive way means that you are behaving this way for your own self-interest, accepting responsibility for your future (it is negative self-interest and fear to opt out of taking responsibility for your future). Your parents might have expected you to go to the university to become a Doctor; and you decided that you wanted to be a Banker instead. Is this being selfish? Or is this the result of well-researched and well thought-out logic and reasoning? Maybe your partner wants a sports car and you want a saloon car, and you get the saloon car. Is this being selfish, or is your choice to have a saloon car more appropriate to your budget and children you may have? I have always believed that a mother should learn to put herself first.

To explain this further, I believe that if a mother of young children looks after herself and does not overdo domestic chores, rests whenever she can, and delegates to others, then she is better equipped for doing this as she is not tired and stretching herself and is therefore able to give 100 percent of her energy to the children, because she has taken care of herself first. How can a frustrated, distraught mother give her children positive nurturing unless she looks after herself first? I accept that this course of action is not always an option. But at all times, I believe you should take care of yourself before you take care of others.

When traveling by air, the flight attendant will take you through the ritual of safety instructions in the event of an emergency. It is interesting to note that when they come to explaining the safety issues for the children, they always emphasize that the parent should put on their life-saving jackets first and then carry out the procedure for the children. It's really the same principle, isn't it? If you see to yourself, those children and people around you will benefit as a result of this self-nurturing. What these examples prove is that being selfish does not necessarily mean that you are obstinate, difficult, and destructive. The opposite of selfish is selfless. You are selfless when you give up what you want for someone else. You are selfless when you let someone else have their own way. You are selfless when you let someone take control of your life. Selflessness is 'self-imposed martyrdom.' Not a nice state to live in!

The question is, 'What are you going to do about this?' You have two options:

Option 1: Stay as you are. You might think that you have managed being this way this far into your life, so why should you change?

Option 2: Decide to retrain your mind and change your negative beliefs so that you can gain self-respect, self-worth, and join the posse of positive, energetic, enthusiastic people who believe that life is adventurous and fun.

It is your choice. Don't be led into doing something that you are not whole-hearted about. If you are coerced into changing yourself by your partner or anyone else, it won't work out because you will be doing it for them and not for you. All personal emotional development only works if you want to embark on the process of change for you.

Examples of the negative elements of selfishness:

- Being selfish is keeping everything for you;
- Being selfish is using others;
- Being selfish is being covetous;
- Being selfish is being spiteful;
- Being selfish is uncaring;
- Being selfish is destructive;

- Being selfish is not considering other people's feelings;
- Being selfish is believing you have the right to do and say anything with no consequences.

Here are some of the positive elements of selfishness:

- You will have the ability to store emotional energy in order to help yourself first and then other people;
- You will treat others with respect;
- You will be able to more easily identify what your partner (and others) need and want from you;
- You will be better placed to look after someone else.

Selfishness as a Facet of Your Personality

Your ego/ personality is made up of many parts. Selfishness is only one of them. Do you know how many parts of your personality there are?

Try to recognize your personality parts with some examples to help you:

- You are loud;
- You are irresponsible;
- Your are lazy;
- You are shy;
- You are emotional;
- You are untidy;
- You are adventurous;
- You are glamorous;

- You are intelligent;
- You are dramatic;
- You are interesting.

There are many more that I am sure you can add to this list. For every example I have given above, there is an opposite, which I will list below, and they are all aspects of who you are:

- You are quiet;
- You are responsible;
- You are active;
- You are outgoing;
- You are unemotional;
- You are messy;
- You are drab;
- You are unintelligent;
- You are boring;
- You are disinterested.

There are aspects of yourself you may not like or accept, but this does not mean that they don't exist. If you want to have a fulfilling relationship with your partner, it will be beneficial for you to uncover and examine which part or parts of your personality you interact with. When you have done this, you will find that you are more at ease and compatible in reacting from that/those particular part(s) of your personality. You will see also that you have only reacted from this part of your personality and have chosen not to react from, or even acknowledge, other elements of your personality.

The lists above identify that if you regard yourself as unemotional, then the other part of your personality is emotional, but have refused subconsciously to accept that you are. When you understand how your behavior is linked to your personality in this way, you will more readily accept how limited your vision is and how narrow-minded you have been in not accepting and acknowledging other parts of your personality and not considering thinking about and operating from these standpoints also.

The ability to see the whole of your personality will enable you to begin interacting from those parts of your personality you have ignored and not given life to. You will be giving yourself the opportunity to compart-mentalize all the different aspects of your personality and be able to call upon a particular aspect of your personality that will be a more appropriate behavior in response to situations that occur.

You may have heard the phrase, 'opposites attract'. This well-worn phrase encapsulates that if you ignore parts of yourself, you will be attracted to these facets of your personality in your partner/others. The traits and qualities you do not recognize and admire in yourself but recognize in your partner or other people are traits you need to nurture and adopt yourself. You will be drawn to these parts of your partner, not realizing that you are in denial of having these parts yourself. When you learn to see and absorb the negative or opposite side to your traits, you will become more understanding and less judgmental of the negative traits in others.

In order to fully experience life, you need to know and understand all the aspects of your personality/ego whether they be good or bad. You need to become aware of all the aspects of your partner's personality, or that of anyone who is close to you, so that you can respond in a sensitive and appropriate way, and also to protective yourself, should you need to. If you are ready to acknowledge that you have a list of negative traits as well as a list of positive traits, it naturally follows on that you will be more understanding and less judgmental of your partner's/others' negative traits, when these traits manifest.

Think about the parts of your partner/other people you don't like. Write them down. Take a good hard look at what you have written and ask yourself, 'Are these traits that I have identified in my partner the same as some of my own traits that I have dismissed?' This concept works on the belief that you draw to you people who are similar to you and also people you can learn from. For instance, the aspects you don't like in your partner's personality are also in your personality. This would suggest that you should address these ignored or dismissed aspects of your personality so that you can become more aware of all your personality traits and more understanding and less judgmental of your partner and others.

Let's take a look at a simple example of the many facets of your personality:

Sober	I am serious, studious, reliable, and easygoing.
Drunk	I am aggressive, argumentative, and difficult to be with.
Normal	I am sensible, level headed, and rational.
Stressed-out	I am tired, fed up, and emotional

These four examples are indications of how many facets there are to your personality.

Exercise: find out more about yourself by identifying as many aspects of your own personality as you can. Be honest with yourself.

If both partners acknowledge you have access to and can use all aspects of your personality, you will be less likely to judge each other during times of conflict. You need to develop a reservoir of reactions and responses to further develop and fulfill your relationship.

Step 7 – 'If Only!'

The 'if only' stage of being stuck on your emotional development path is like constantly living in a dream world.

Living in the Dream World

Here are some examples:

- If only I was rich!
- If only I was pretty/handsome!
- If only I was clever!
- If only I was liked!
- If only I had been better educated!
- If only I hadn't experienced emotionally difficult times in my life!
- If only my children were respectful!
- If only my partner was more understanding!
- If only I wasn't in love with someone other than my partner!
- If only I could have the life I crave for!
- If only I was A or B (other than yourself)!
- If only there wasn't a black cloud over me!
- If only I hadn't made mistakes!
- If only I had listened to my parents!

- If only I had been shown more love!

And on and on we go. What a bore! What a copout! How long can someone live in this dream state? Let's get real. Let's accept who we are and be done with this dreaming. For all of these statements, write down your answers; an example of what I mean is, 'If only I was rich!' OK so if you were rich, what would that do for you? Yes, you could buy a better house. *Yes*, you could buy a better car. *Yes*, you could buy designer clothes. *Yes*, you could have expensive holidays. *Yes, yes, yes*, you could do all these things. Ask yourself how long you would remain happy. You would eventually get bored because you still have to live with who you are. Money can change your living circumstances, but it can't change your inner thoughts or your personality. You would have different problems if you were rich, for example:

- You would wonder if people were nice to you because you had money;
- You would wonder if you were truly attractive or only being fancied because of your money;
- You would wonder people's motives for everything they did and said;
- You would be lonely if you thought all this stuff;
- You would lose your friends because they couldn't keep up with you or because you were away on holidays so much that they never got to see you;
- You would wonder if your old friends expected you to buy all the drinks on a night out;

- You would wonder what your old friends think of you now.

Within every aspect of your dream state, there would be problems of a different sort, but problems nonetheless. The 'if only' questions are a road to emotional pain. To continue on this road is not staying in reality. It's perfectly ok for you to dream occasionally, but to live in a dream state because you are grossly unhappy with your real state can be the start of serious mental health problems. However, there is a positive side to 'dreaming'.

Here are some examples of positive dreaming:

- In your dreams, you can aspire to be anyone and do anything;
- In your dreams, you have the capacity to achieve your objective;
- In your dreams, you can have answers to real-life problems;
- In your dreams, you can be happy;
- In your dreams, you can be confident;
- In your dreams, you can be honest;
- In your dreams, you might be able to see what it is you really want.

Decide to write down the dreams you remember. With practice you can remember your dreams. When you have done this, ask yourself if you can make your dreams come true.

Positive dreaming can assist you in getting what you want as it provides you with a vision of how you want

your life to be. Don't disregard your positive dreams for
these can be used as a foundation to build upon.

Cosmic Ordering

Cosmic Ordering is a New Age belief whereby an
individual spiritually connects to the *cosmos* to reveal
their deepest desires, with the belief that the cosmos
will use its energy to turn these desires into a reality.
Cosmic ordering is not tied to the dogma of any one
specific belief system or faith, although it does share
similarities. The act of cosmic ordering can be likened
to prayer, because it involves an individual communi-
cating with the cosmos. Cosmic ordering also shares
similarities with goal setting, because it involves the
pursuit of a specific objective.'

What is so wrong with 'cosmic ordering?' Isn't it just
the same as a wish list, a dream of how you want your
life to be? We are told that the way to 'cosmic order' is
to write what you want in your life on a piece of paper
and place it under your pillow. Isn't that similar to
saying a prayer? Isn't that similar to believing that your
thoughts and actions can result in good and bad karma
coming back to you? Isn't that similar to being positive?
Isn't that similar to changing your negative belief
patterns and replacing them with positive belief patterns?

Professional psychologists and other clinical profes-
sionals, generally, debunk the idea of comic ordering,
not believing that the cosmos listens to private requests
and granting them. Their theory is that there are people
who know exactly what they want in life and that they
recognize and grasp opportunities as they come along. I
agree with this theory. I believe that you can decide

what you want and also believe that you will get it. I believe that you should try to live in the moment and should remember that the thoughts you have today create your tomorrow. I subscribe to the belief that what you dream today you can achieve tomorrow.

Cosmic ordering is essentially acknowledging and asking for what you want in your life. In acknowledging your thoughts, you are already 'placing an order', 'saying a prayer', 'stating an objective'. Whichever way you look at it, this is personal, positive acknowledgement for you alone to achieve your heart's desire. It's similar to the premise of 'act happy and you become happy'; it's a way of becoming what you most desire now and gives you encouragement to achieving what you might have believed was the impossible. Where you are, and where you go, depends only on you. By believing that you can do it, you are half way there to achieving it.

Step 8 – 'I Should Be Doing Something Else With My Time'

Yes, you should be doing something else with your time instead of rummaging around in your negative memory box, looking for stuff that holds you back from experiencing life. You should be actually taking part in life—doing things, feeling things, learning things.

If Only...

When you are thinking 'if only,' you are focusing on the negative aspects in your life and particularly in your relationships. In any marriage/partnership, it is important to realize and understand that there are some negative aspects, because no one is perfect. It is more important, however, that you focus on all the positive aspects in your relationship. In order to have the relationship you want, you must first change the way you look at life in general. Being in your dream state takes you out of reality and can be destructive in that continually dreaming the 'if only' scenario reinforces what you haven't got and want desperately. Your dream state can make you frustrated and totally unhappy with what you have now. Always reinforcing the negative will not only destroy you emotionally, but it will also destroy your relationship. As stated in Step 7, there is a positive side to 'dreaming'.

Start writing a list on what you most admire about the people who are close to you. Focus on the 'here and now' and learn what advantages there are when you examine the good aspects of what you've got.

Here are some examples to help you:

- My partner is helpful;
- My family are supportive;
- My friends are reliable and kind.

The Partner of Your Dreams

Just these three things alone is a good place to start re-evaluating your relationship and your life. Just imagine for a minute that you had the man or woman of your dream. You must have imagined this scenario a thousand times. Now let's get real and look at it again. However wonderful this man or woman is, they will bring into a relationship all their past and present emotional baggage. This person will have his/her own list of dislikes that you will have to learn to accept and overcome. Sit down and really think this through. Get real with your observations. It's only an exercise to get your mind working, isn't it? Write down the traits of your ideal partner and on the opposite page, write down a list of what is most likely his/her faults.

An example:

First page	Second page
I want my man to be wealthy.	This might mean that he will be spending a lot of time at the office or traveling; so loneliness jumps out to bite you.
I want my woman to be glamorous.	Glamorous women spend a long time looking after themselves and spend a lot of money achieving the right look—'superficial and frivolous' leaps to the front of my mind; and also their partner's needs will always be second.

When you actually delve deeper into your dream, you will discover that actually it is only a dream and thank God for that. I am sure you have heard the expression, *'better the devil you know rather than the devil you don't know'*. Do you feel better after this exercise? You should be reassured.

Being with your present partner might be boring sometimes; however, you have the choice to do something to stop being bored. Think of different activities you could both become involved in. Learn to love your partner the way he/she is rather than dreaming what you would like them to be.

> Every adversity, every failure, and every heartache, carries with it the Seed of an equivalent or greater Benefit.
>
> Napoleon Hill

When you stop learning and changing, you stop living and feeling. The 'if only path' is a road to nowhere. Stop daydreaming and start living.

What could you do with your time?

If that is an issue, let's look at the following suggestions:

- You could go on a course to learn something new;
- You could spend more time with your family and friends;
- You could plan a holiday;
- You could do some home decorating;
- You could take up gardening;
- You could learn computer skills and surf the net;
- You could learn to have fun. Remember fun?
- You could invest in yourself, look after yourself, and have a makeover for the fun of it;
- You could learn how to be responsible;
- You could learn how to be more involved with your partner (sharing the domestic chores, finances, hobbies, etc);
- You could learn to like yourself by being kind to yourself and treating yourself. Rewards always make you feel better (in the short term).

Step 9 – How Does Guilt Differ From Shame?

Guilt and shame are closely related, they are almost blood brothers. A simple explanation is that you 'feel guilty for what you do and you feel shame for what you are'. Shame in this instance comes out much worse than guilt because shame is what you feel and guilt is a reaction to what you've done. That which you have done can be undone by thinking differently and undoing the bad you believe you did. If you feel both guilt and shame then your idea of who you really are, your basic nature, is at an all time low and this, obviously, can affect you greatly in particular with your partner. You can believe that you are bad through and through.

Dictionary definition of 'Shame': "a painful feeling arising from the consciousness of something dishonorable, improper, ridiculous etc, done by oneself or another."

Shame identifies what is intrinsically wrong with you. It looks inside you and makes you feel bad about yourself. Shame is different from guilt. Guilt is the unpleasant feeling you experience when you sabotage your core beliefs. You can do something about guilt. You can change your behavior. In biblical terms, you can repent. But shame goes deeper than guilt. It attacks the essence of your identify. I read an article by the psychologist Norman Wright, who stated, "Guilt says 'I have made a mistake;' shame says 'I am a mistake.'"

Here are some examples of how shame can affect you:

- You will not take part in social occasions;
- You will avoid people;
- You will be withdrawn;
- You will be defensive;
- You will be aggressive;
- You will display bad behavior;
- You will enlarge conflict;
- You will attack others before they attack you;
- You will try to break people down (by put downs, humiliating, etc.,) in order to rise above them. This will provide short-term relief;
- You will project your faults on other people;
- You will be too nice and self-sacrificial to hide your feeling of shame;
- You will believe that whatever to do it is always wrong.

How to Overcome Shame

Following is a list of some of the causes of shame:

- Your lack of trust in yourself;
- Your lack of trust in your partner, family, friends;
- Your memory box, which encompasses your early-learning, negative experiences;

- Not accepting and overcoming past emotional hurts;
- Your depressive, negative thoughts;
- Your fear of being rejected by your partner or others;
- Being unable to let go of past emotional pain;
- Being unable to forgive significant people who you believe have caused you emotional hurt.

And many more, that will be unique to each of you reading this book.

Now let's take a look at some of the root causes of guilt:

- Believing your negative thought process;
- Your drive to become perfect (if you don't reach the standard you set for yourself, you will feel guilty about this) ;
- Taking personal responsibility for everyone's happiness;
- Based in your dislike and resentment of your partner or others;
- That you know that you manipulate your partner or others;
- Your knowledge that you have said or done something that is detrimental to your partner or others.

This list is endless and will be different for each of you.

Dealing With Causes of Guilt and Shame

You can deal with the cause of guilt and shame by confronting your past issues and childhood environment. When a child is raised by role models who are emotionally aware, the experience of shame passed on to the child is healthy, strong, and nourishing. When a child is brought up by role models who are ashamed, the shame they pass on to their child is toxic (poisonous).

In order for you to be clear in your understanding of how past experiences affect you as an adult, try the following:

Name a problem that you are currently experiencing guilt and/or shame about;

- Ask yourself whether you are responsible for this problem;
- Ask yourself who else could be responsible for this problem;
- Ask yourself whether you have made this problem worse by making it bigger than it really is;
- Ask yourself if your current problem reminds you of a similar problem you remember from your childhood;
- Ask yourself how this childhood problem was resolved;
- Ask yourself whether you are happy, now that you are an adult and with hindsight, with the way the problem in your childhood was dealt with, and resolved;
- Ask yourself if there are any similarities between the way you are dealing with your current problem and the way you remember your childhood problem was processed and resolved;

- Ask yourself if it is appropriate to solve your current problem by using the same strategy that your role models used to resolve the childhood problem you have remembered;
- Ask yourself on a scale from 1 to 10, 10 being very bad, how much guilt and shame you feel with regard to your current problem;
- Ask yourself if the fact that you feel guilt and shame makes the problem easier or worse for you;
- Ask yourself how you would feel if you did not experience guilt and shame with regard to this problem.
- Ask yourself how you would deal with your current problem without feeling guilt and shame.

This exercise is aimed at helping you identify how you might be unconsciously linking in to your early learning experiences and a negative belief system used by your role models. Now ask yourself, 'Should I continue with this negative belief pattern and thought process that has outlived its usefulness?' I believe you will come to the conclusion that your old habit is unhelpful in resolving current issues.

I would like you to look again at the last question in the series of questions. The question is, 'Ask yourself how you would deal with your current problem without feeling guilt and shame'.

- Think about feeling free of guilt and shame;
- Close your eyes and imagine being completely free of these disabling irrational emotions with your current problem.

- Stay in the frame of mind which has dismissed your feelings of guilt and shame.

- Focus on the new feeling of freedom that is without guilt and shame. It feels good, doesn't it?

- Next, make a conscious choice to let go of the guilt and shame with regard to this problem.

Learn and understand that guilt and shame stop you from dealing with the problem. They are the barriers that disable your progress in resolving this and any problem. Ask yourself, 'How can I resolve this and any problem if I put myself in the position of being the problem?' The answer is that you cannot successfully resolve a problem if you feel guilty and ashamed. Your negative belief system that has been stored in your memory box will always link you to resolving any problem via the route of negativity. You will not resolve a problem by being negative and feeling negative emotions.

I hope that this exercise has helped you acknowledge your old negative belief system and has shown you that it is no longer helpful for you to use this method of problem-solving. Everyone has a belief system that was started in childhood. The process of resolving a problem in your past by your role models might have been entirely productive during that time. But as you move from childhood to adulthood, your thought process might no longer be of any value or use to you. Every one of us has to reassess our early learning skills and adapt them so that they are appropriate in the here and now.

What If You Never Feel Guilt?

There are some people who never feel guilty. Perhaps you have heard the popular term, 'I don't do guilt' on some reality TV shows. That is not to say that these people are necessarily psychopathic and dangerous; it's just that they have made a decision not to worry about something they have said or done or cannot change. They don't feel guilty because prior to doing or saying something that might be considered unpopular to many, they have researched and analyzed the situation they are in and have made a conscious decision to move forward in the way that they feel is appropriate for them, regardless of their partner's opinion. Whereas other people might feel tremendous guilt over the same issue, the people who do not feel guilt are able to justify their speech and actions and believe they are redeemed via this route as it is preferable to following the honesty trail that would, they believe, inevitably lead to quarrels, rows, disagreements, and separations.

My own research has uncovered that some people who live in emotionally difficult relationships handle their partner by becoming secretive and dishonest. The people who adopt this method of coping are afraid to be upfront and open with their partner and feel that they have been forced to become underhanded in order not to upset their partner and the equilibrium of the household. They have learned that being honest and open with their partner produces reactions of hostility, anger, and behavior that have long-reaching consequences. Sometimes it is appropriate to keep some information to yourself, particularly if the issues are about jealousy or anger (emotional abuse). Yes, this is deceptive behavior, but the reason that some people reach this conclusion is usually because they have tried everything else and this way of coping is a last resort to stay in the relationship. This method appears to be a simpler, non-confrontational way of warding off quarrels and arguments. I have urged women who handle their relationships in this way to ask themselves, 'Is there any need to discuss this issue with my partner?' If the honest answer is 'no', then don't.

I believe that before reacting to a situation or voicing an opinion that presents itself with your partner, you should first of all check out whether what you are about to say is pertinent to the discussion. If it isn't pertinent, it's impertinent; if it isn't appropriate, it's inappropriate; if it isn't relevant, it's irrelevant. This is a good yardstick to use before entering into a debate that could spiral out of control. This method of coping and behaving will offset many squabbles and petty arguments.

Step 10 – A Fresh Start in a Conscious Marriage

Constant conflict between partners will eventually destroy a relationship. Guilt, fear, insecurity, lack of communication will be at the root of disharmony and discontentment. The key to a better relationship, one without guilt, is to get back to the basic stuff that made you initially fall in love with each other.

Life, after being successful at ditching guilt, is filled with promise. It is an opportunity for two people to cast off old habits and develop healthy emotional patterns. Let us take a look at what you have learned so far:

- That there is false guilt and true guilt;
- How to identify the origin of your guilt (where it came from);
- About role models;
- The difference between guilt and shame;
- The many types of emotional guilt;
- The skills needed to overcome guilt;
- About the role of a victim/perpetrator/guilty one;
- About the negative and positive aspects of guilt;
- Cosmic ordering (dreaming);

- Negative and positive selfishness.

These are some of the things that this book has helped you to look at. The next thing on the agenda is to make a plan.

Here are some examples of what your plan should contain?

- Your objective (an objective is something you have jointly agreed to aim for);
- Specifics on what you both want to achieve;
- A timescale to achieving your objective;
- Allowance for delays in meeting your objective;
- A short list of targets on your way to reaching your objective (targets are identified as small changes you intend to make in your relationship with your partner or others);
- Reflect possible changes that might be necessary;
- A confirmation of your commitment to these tasks.

Guilt

Guilt is a killer
It kills true love
It's sly and contagious
And it's very bad

Guilt erodes a relationship
It destroys the soul
It damages everything
With nothing to show

How can I stop it?
It's ruining my life!
I try to hold on
to put up a fight

The battle is lost
What can I do?
It has me in its grip
I depend on you

I yearn for your arms
To hold me again
To tell me you love me
That it's not all in vain

The guilt is receding
I think it has gone
Thank you for helping
I know I was wrong

I am starting afresh
Leaving the past behind
The future is before me
I have a new mind

A mind that is free of guilt and of shame
A mind that accepts and moves on from blame

Bibliography

Amen, D. G. (1998). *Change your brain, change your life: The breakthrough program for conquering anxiety, depression, obsessiveness, anger, and impulsiveness.* New York: Times Books.

Brady, T. (2007). *Regaining control: When love becomes a prison.* Ann Arbor, MI: Loving Healing Press.

Byrne, R. (2006). *Secret: Self-help, spiritual, the book is based on the law of attraction.* : Australia: Atria Books, Beyond Words Publishing

Carson, R.D. (1983). *Taming Your gremlin: A guide to enjoying yourself.* Dallas, The Family Resource

Covey, S. (1990). *The 7 habits of highly effective people.* A fireside book. New York: Simon & Schuster.

Davies, L. (1992) *Allies in healing: When the person you love was sexually abused as a child.* San Francisco: Harper Perennial

Dickson, A., & Charlesworth, K. (1982). *A woman in your own right: Assertiveness and you.* London: Quartet.

Dyer, W. (1979). *Pulling your own strings.* New York: Avon Books

Greist, J. H., Jefferson, J. W., & Marks, I. M. (1986). *Anxiety and its treatment: Help is available : advice from three leading psychiatrists in the field of anxiety treatment*. Washington, DC: American Psychiatric Press.

Goleman, D. (1995). *Emotional intelligence*. New York: Bantam Books.

Gray, J. (1998) *Men are from Mars, Women are from Venus*. Harper Collins

Jeffers, S. J. (1996). *End the struggle and dance with life: How to build yourself up when the world gets you down*. New York: St. Martin's Press.

Jeffers, S. (1997). *Feel the fear and do it anyway: How to turn your fear and indecision into confidence and action*. London: Rider.

Keith, K. M. (2002). *Anyway: The paradoxical commandments: finding personal meaning in a crazy world*. New York: Putnam.

Kennerley, Helen (1997). *Overcoming anxiety: A self-help guide using cognitive behavioural techniques*. Great Britain: Robinson Publishing Ltd

Klagasbrun, Francine (1985). *Married people: Staying together in the age of divorce*. New York: Bantam Books

Lew, M. (1990). *Victims no longer: Men recovering from incest and other sexual child abuse*. New York: Perennial Library.

McKenna, P., & Willbourn, H. (2006). *I can mend your broken heart*. London: Bantam.

McKay, M., Davis, M., & Fanning, P. (2009). *Messages: The communication skills book.* Oakland, Calif: New Harbinger Publications.

Murphy, J. G. (2005). *Getting even: Forgiveness and its limits.* New York: Oxford University Press.

Norwood, R. (1985). *Women who love too much: When you keep wishing and hoping he'll change.* Los Angeles: J.P. Tarcher.

Norwood, R. (1994). *Why me, why this, why now: A guide to answering life's toughest questions.* New York: C. Southern Books

Pease, B., & Pease, A. (2000). *Why men don't listen & women can't read maps: How we're different and what to do about it.* New York, NY: Welcome Rain

Randall, P. (2001). *Bullying in adulthood: Assessing the bullies and their victims.* New York: Brunner-Routledge.

Rosellini, G. & Worden, M. (1990). *Barriers to Intimacy: For people torn by addiction and compulsive behaviour:* USA: Ballantine Books

Smith, M. J. (1975). *When I say no, I feel guilty: How to cope--using the skills of systematic assertive therapy.* New York: Dial Press.

Volkman, M. (2005) *Life Skills: Improve the Quality of Your Life with Metapsychology.* Loving Healing Press: Ann Arbor, MI.

About the Author

Lynda Bevan lives in a picturesque village in South Wales, United Kingdom. She is 59 years of age, married for the third time, with three (adult) children. During her teens and early twenties, she pursued and enjoyed acting and taught drama at local Youth Centers.

Her 22-year career has involved working in the area of mental health, with the two major care agencies in the UK, Social Services and the National Health Service.

After the birth of her third child, and with her second marriage ending, she became employed by Social Services and climbed through the ranks to senior management level with some speed.

During her career with Social Services, she developed a passion for counseling and psychotherapy and worked extensively with mental health patients within the organization, setting up counseling projects in Health-care Centers. The task was to tackle the issue of doctors who inappropriately referred patients to Psychiatric Hospitals for therapy when they had experienced events that arise in normal everyday life, e.g., divorce, anxiety, depression, bereavement, stress, loss of role. It was during this time that she became involved in marital/ relationship counseling and, coincidentally, was experiencing difficulties within her own relationship. The experience of working in this environment, and her own relationship issues, enabled Lynda to be innovative; creating methods of coping and developing strategies that enabled her and her patients to live within their problematic relationships. These strategies were devised and offered to patients who had clearly identified that they did not want to separate or proceed with the divorce process.

After taking early retirement from Social Services, she became employed by the National Health Service as a Counselor in the Primary Healthcare Setting. During this period in her career, she began using the strategies she had developed with patients who were referred for relationship counseling and who did not want to end their partnership/ marriage. These strategies have been used extensively over a ten-year period with impressive results.

Lynda is presently employed as a Manager of a charity that supports people who are HIV positive. She is also the Resident Relationship Counselor on Swansea Sound Radio.

Index

Life Without Jealousy

A Practical Guide

LYNDA BEVAN

Ask yourself...

- Do you feel the need to be frequently checking up on your partner?
- Are you suspicious when you meet new people?
- Do you often question your partner about where they are going and who they are seeing?
- Do you withdraw from your partner without giving an explanation as to why you doing this?
- Do you make all of the social arrangements for your partner's life?
- Have you ever feigned illness to keep your partner at home?
- Are you frightened of being unable to survive without your partner?
- Do you examine on your partner's phone records, emails, or text messages "just in case"?
- Do you put your partner down over small details or infractions of agreements?

If you answered YES to more than one of these questions, then this book is for you.

This is the book to help you overcome this unwanted emotion. You will embark on a journey to discover the many types of jealousy. You can use this book as a manual to overcome emotional insecurity issues and to give you a clearer perspective on the emotion of jealousy. By engaging with the exercises with this book, you'll be able to see yourself as you really are and further exercises will assist you in eliminating your jealous thoughts and behavior.

"I truly feel that every individual who is dealing with issues of some form of jealousy will greatly benefit from reading *Life Without Jealousy* by Lynda Bevan. This includes people who are not jealous themselves but are being affected by others who are. Learning to understand it, overcome it, and gain effective new ways to communicate will greatly improve the quality of our lives."

--Paige Lovitt, *Reader Views*

Learn more at **www.LyndaBevan.com**

Book #4 in the 10-Step Empowerment Series
from Loving Healing Press
www.LovingHealing.com

FAMILY & RELATIONSHIPS / Love & Romance
Psychology : Emotions

Lightning Source UK Ltd.
Milton Keynes UK
UKOW04f1203060215

245816UK00001B/48/P